W9-BEA-742

The Story of
OLD IRONSIDES

By Norman Richards

Illustrated by Tom Dunnington

CHILDRENS PRESS, CHICAGO

5 6 7 8 9 10 11 12 13 14 15 R 75

Library of Congress Catalog Card Number: 67-20099
Copyright ©, 1967, Childrens Press, Inc.
All rights reserved. Printed in the U.S.A.
Published simultaneously in Canada

When the United States was very young it did not have many people. It was not a big, powerful nation as it is today. The rulers of some of the older countries cared very little about the rights of Americans.

When American merchants tried to trade peacefully in Europe and North Africa, their ships were raided and sometimes captured. When they sailed past Gibraltar into the Mediterranean Sea, they were chased by pirates from the Barbary Coast nations of Morocco, Algiers, Tunis and Tripoli. Sometimes they could sail faster and escape, but often their ships were captured.

The pirates brought the captured ships to their rulers. The American crewmen were thrown into prison or forced to work as slaves.

The United States government could do nothing about this. Without a navy the government could not protect American ships.

President George Washington told the men in Congress about the problem and warned, "If we desire to avoid insult, we must repel it."

But Congress had little money to spend on defense. The leaders said, "We are a peaceful country. Let us pay the rulers of the Barbary Coast a sum of money for the privilege of sailing into the Mediterranean."

George Washington told them, "Once the pirates know they can force us to pay, they will demand more. We should begin to build a navy."

The men in Congress reached a compromise. A treaty was signed with the Dey of Algiers, the most powerful Barbary ruler. He agreed to let American ships pass safely if the United States paid him a large sum of money every year.

At the same time, Congress voted to build six big warships. Three were to be built immediately. The other three would be built only if peace could not be kept. The men in Congress said, "Now we are at peace, and we are safe."

As time passed, Americans found out that George Washington was right. The United States could not defend itself without a navy. American ships were insulted on the high seas.

An insult came from France, which had been friendly with America before. England and France were at war with each other. France thought

American merchant ships were bringing war supplies to England when they sailed into English ports to trade. French warships shot at the American ships. Sometimes they captured them and took them to French ports.

The American representative in Paris, Charles Pinckney, complained to the men in the French government. These leaders told him that France would give the captured ships back if the Americans paid them a large sum of money as a tribute. This tribute would protect American ships.

Charles Pinckney was proud of his young country. He was angry at this demand. He said if

America had to spend any more money, they should spend it to defend themselves from other countries.

"Millions for defense, but not one cent for tribute!" he shouted.

The people in America agreed with him. They held large gatherings in the streets of cities. They declared, "The seas are free and we must be allowed to sail in peace. Build the navy!"

When the leaders in Congress heard what the people wanted, they could not refuse. They voted to build the other three warships in addition to the three already completed.

Skilled carpenters brought their tools to the shipyards to work on the new ships. The first to be completed was named the *United States*. It was launched at Philadelphia. The second was the *Constellation*, built at Baltimore. The third was the *Constitution*, constructed at Boston.

The men who built the *Constitution* wanted her to be the finest warship ever seen. She was a type known as a frigate, which was one of the largest kinds of fighting ships in those days.

Sailmakers worked in the sunshine at the Boston shipyard, sewing huge square, canvas sails together with large needles. They made 72 sails for the *Constitution,* enough to cover an acre of ground.

Lumbermen brought the finest planks of live oak and red cedar. Carpenters steamed them over fires and bent them to fit the curve of the hull of the ship. They fastened the planks with round wooden pegs. To protect the sides of the *Constitution* against enemy cannon, they added to the outside huge oak planks 21 inches thick.

Paul Revere, the famous patriot and metal smith, made a copper covering for the part of the ship below the water line. The men in his copper mill made large plates of copper and bolts with which to fasten them onto the ship's hull.

Lumbermen searched the forests for the tallest, straightest trees for the *Constitution's* three masts. The foremast, in the bow or front, was over 200 feet tall. The mainmast, amidships was 233 feet tall. The mizzenmast, in the stern or rear, was 180 feet tall. Each mast was built in three sections.

The *Constitution* was a square-rigger. Her many sails hung from yardarms at right angles to the masts.

The builders designed the ship for speed. They gave it more than the usual number of sails to catch the wind. They made the hull streamlined to cut through the water easily.

Gunsmiths installed 44 big cannon on the frigate. The shiny barrels poked out of square holes in the ship's sides. The new vessel's gunners were proud of their cannon and they practiced faithfully to become expert shots.

It was a proud day for Americans in July, 1797 when the *Constitution* sailed out of Boston for the first time. Crowds of men, women and children lined the harbor to watch. Shopkeepers left their stores. Blacksmiths left their forges and tools. Candlemakers left the tallow in their molds and hurried to the harbor. Everyone wanted to see the new fighting ship embark on her first voyage.

The people cheered as the big frigate sailed out of the harbor, flags flying in the breeze. Most of her crew of 400 officers and men stood on deck. They may not have guessed it at the time, but the *Constitution* was to become the most famous ship in American history.

France soon agreed to stop capturing American ships. But the Barbary rulers began to seize merchant ships again.

But this time the American people had a navy. Congress decided to send a powerful squadron of six ships to the Barbary Coast. Commodore Edward Preble, who had fought in the War for Independence, was the commander. He chose the new ship *Constitution* as his flagship.

Commodore Preble was a man of action. The first thing he did when he reached the Mediterranean was to straighten out a dispute with the Emperor of Morocco. The Emperor was holding the American consul prisoner in his capital city of Tangier. Preble decided to force him to release the American official.

The *Constitution* and two other ships sailed boldly into the harbor at Tangier. Pirate guns were pointed at the ships, but the American guns were pointed at the city, too.

Preble took only two men with him when he went to visit the Emperor at his castle. When he left the *Constitution* he told his men, "If the least injury is offered to any American, attack the city and the Emperor's castle with all your guns. Don't worry about my safety."

"Aye, Aye, sir," replied the crewmen.

When Preble and his two men approached the Emperor they were told to kneel.

"Americans do not kneel to any man," Preble declared.

The angry Emperor threatened to hold Preble as a prisoner. But the Commodore replied grimly, "If you do, the guns of the *Constitution* and my other ships will destroy your castle and your whole city."

The Emperor's men had told him about the powerful American warships. The Americans were not easy prey for his pirates any longer. Seeing that he could not frighten Preble, he backed down. He released the American consul from prison and promised not to capture any more ships.

But some of the other pirate leaders of the Barbary Coast still had to be convinced that the Americans intended to defend themselves. One of the most powerful of these was the ruler of Tripoli, called the Bashaw of Tripoli. He continued to demand that America pay tribute or have its ships seized.

The Bashaw's city of Tripoli was defended by 115 cannon overlooking the harbor, 22 gunboats and an army of 25,000 soldiers. But this did not frighten Preble. He ordered the *Constitution* and the other ships of his squadron to blockade the city. The ships anchored outside the harbor and refused to let the pirate ships go in or out of it. The blockade lasted several months, and the Americans sank and captured many of the enemy gunboats. Twice Preble sailed the *Constitution* right into the harbor, guns blazing. The mighty ship bombarded the city and the batteries of guns on shore. Both times it escaped without damage.

The Tripoli pirates feared the big frigate, and the Bashaw finally saw that he could not win. He agreed to stop demanding tribute. He promised to let American merchant ships sail in peace.

Now there remained only one Barbary Coast leader who did not respect the rights of American ships. He was called the Bey of Tunis. But he quickly changed his mind when the *Constitution* and the other warships sailed into his city's harbor with guns ready. A message was delivered from the *Constitution*: "If you do not keep the peace, you will feel the vengeance of the American squadron now in the harbor." The Bey agreed to be peaceful, and American vessels were able to sail the Mediterranean Sea in safety from that time on.

The fame of the *Constitution* spread. The American people had gained respect from other nations. They were proud of their great warship. But the leaders of one great nation, Great Britain, laughed at America as a young upstart. Great Britain had the mightiest navy in the world, with more than 600 ships. The British were at war with France and they needed many sailors for their ships.

They began stopping American merchant vessels at sea to look for English sailors who had run away. But instead of taking only Englishmen found on American ships, they would also capture Americans. They forced the American seamen to work on their ships. They refused to allow them to prove they were American citizens. They refused to listen to the protests of the United States government.

The leaders in America finally decided that they must defend their rights once more. Congress declared war on Great Britain in 1812. The British laughed at the small American army and navy.

When they heard about the *Constitution's* victories on the Barbary Coast, they were not impressed. They said, "The ship is a bundle of pine boards, sailing under a bit of striped bunting." They bragged that British ships would drive the American frigate from the ocean.

One of the British naval officers who laughed at

the American navy was Captain James Dacres. He was a skilled naval leader who commanded a large frigate called the *Guerriere*. When he captured an American ship, he released the crew with a message to bring back to American ports: "I will be happy to meet with the captain of any American frigate who dares to do battle."

One man who dared was Captain Isaac Hull, who was now captain of the *Constitution*. He was a daring, able mariner who loved his country. He wanted to defeat the British so they would stop ignoring the rights of Americans at sea.

Captain Hull knew the *Constitution* was faster than most warships. He knew how to maneuver the big ship beautifully. He ordered his gunners to practice until they were the most accurate gunners in the world. He was confident that his ship could overtake most ships at sea and defeat them.

At last, one sunny afternoon, the *Constitution* met *Guerriere* far out at sea. "Clear the decks for action!" Hull ordered.

"All hands to quarters!" yelled the chief boatswain's mate. Gun crewmen rushed to their places beside their cannon. Sailors formed a line to pass ammunition along to the gunners. Drummer boys beat a battle call on their drums to alert everybody on board. The two ships drew closer to each other.

"Break out the colors!" Hull ordered. The American flag was displayed on a mast to show the British that it was an American warship. Captain Dacres responded by running up the British flag on the *Guerriere*.

Dacres was eager to start fighting. He ordered the gunners on the British ship to fire while the frigates were still quite a distance apart. The cannon balls fell in the water.

Hull decided to wait until the vessels were close together and then fire with every gun he had. The officer in charge of the gun crews asked permission to fire as the ships came closer together.

"Not yet," Hull replied. He stood on the quarterdeck, watching the enemy ship as it fired at the *Constitution*. Some of the shots hit the ship.

At last, when the ships were very close, Hull shouted, "Now, fire with everything you have!" The *Constitution's* cannon went off with a great roar. Smoke rose in the air. The American gunners were more accurate than the British. The three masts of the *Guerriere* crashed to the deck in a tangle of canvas and lines.

The *Constitution's* thick oak planks protected its sides, and many British cannon balls bounced off them. When one of the American seamen saw this he shouted, "Hurrah! Her sides are made of iron!" Soon other sailors took up the cheer, and after that sailors called the ship *Old Ironsides*.

With all its masts shot off, the *Guerriere* was helpless in the water. Without sails, it could not move. Finally, Dacres surrendered to Hull. The British flag was taken down, which was a signal of surrender. The British crew were taken on board the *Constitution* as prisoners, and American sailors set fire to the *Guerriere*. As the huge British frigate burned and sank into the sea, Hull set sail for Boston to tell about his victory.

The American people had been discouraged with the war. American forces had not won many victories against the much larger forces of Great Britain. But when they heard the news of *Old Ironsides* defeating a proud British warship, they were overjoyed. Great parades were held for Isaac Hull in Boston, New York and Philadelphia. Congress voted to give him a special hero's medal.

The victory gave the American people new spirit. *Old Ironsides* went on to win some other important battles in the war, too. The proud British Navy learned to respect this great warship and they stopped laughing about the American Navy. The two nations finally signed a peace treaty and the war ended. The British agreed to respect the rights of American seamen and promised to leave their ships alone. Once again, *Old Ironsides* had earned respect for America with other nations. And it had made the citizens feel proud and patriotic.

Long years of peace followed, and the *Constitution* had few duties. When the frigate was about thirty years old, its timbers were rotting and it needed a lot of repairs. The officials in the Navy Department knew that it would cost more to repair the old ship than it would to build a brand new one.

They felt it would be better to spend the money on a new ship. So they ordered the *Constitution* to be broken up and destroyed.

When the newspapers published this news, a young Boston student named Oliver Wendell Holmes was very upset. He had heard about the great victories of *Old Ironsides*. He was proud of this great ship and hated to see it destroyed.

"It should be kept so the American people can see it as a reminder of their country's history," he declared.

He sat down and wrote a poem called "Old Ironsides." In the poem he was saying, "It is a great ship, but if the government wants to destroy it, go ahead and destroy it." He sent it to the newspapers and they published it. He hoped the public would get upset when they read the poem. He wanted them to protest to the officials in Washington. The poem went like this:

Ay, tear her tattered ensign down!
Long has it waved on high,
And many an eye has danced to see
That banner in the sky;
Beneath it rung the battle shout,
And burst the cannon's roar:
The meteor of the ocean air
Shall sweep the clouds no more!

Her deck, once red with heroes' blood,
Where knelt the vanquished foe,
When winds were hurrying o'er the flood
And waves were white below.
No more shall feel the victor's tread,
Or know the conquered knee:
The harpies of the shore shall pluck
The eagle of the sea!

O, better that her shattered hulk
Should sink beneath the wave;
Her thunders shook the mighty deep,
And there should be her grave;
Nail to the mast her holy flag,
Set every threadbare sail,
And give her to the god of storms,
The lightning and the gale!

When people read the poem in the newspapers, they protested immediately. Thousands of letters were mailed to the Navy Department in Washington. The officials decided that *Old Ironsides* was too important to the people to be scrapped. It was a symbol of American courage and patriotism.

A new order was issued: repair the *Constitution*. Shortly afterward, a great ceremony was held at the Boston Navy Yard. *Old Ironsides* was towed into a drydock to be rebuilt. Crowds of people cheered as old Captain Isaac Hull took command once more when the great warship entered the drydock. Vice-president Martin Van Buren made a speech about the *Constitution's* glorious past.

Old timbers were taken out and replaced with new ones the same size. New sails were sewn and fitted in place. At last, *Old Ironsides* sailed forth again, as good as new.

The ship was used as a training vessel for many years. Many a young Navy man learned to sail on the great vessel. It sailed all over the world on training cruises. Finally, after many years, it was moored at Boston where visitors could see it.

More than a hundred years had passed since *Old Ironsides* had won its glory in battle. Once again its timbers had rotted, and it was unsafe to sail at sea. People wanted to repair the ship again, so that it could visit other American cities as a symbol of history. But the Secretary of the Navy found that it would cost a half million dollars to make it seaworthy. The government did not have enough money to make the repairs.

Some citizens said, "If the government doesn't have the money, the people will raise it."

Others said, "Let the school children help by sending pennies."

School children all over America brought pennies for *Old Ironsides*. More than five million of them contributed. Adults sent in money, too.

When there was enough money, the *Constitution* was completely rebuilt again. New timbers were put in and it was freshly painted. Once again the old ship looked exactly as it did in its fighting days.

Today *Old Ironsides* is in the Boston Navy Yard. It is officially an active warship of the United States Navy, and it is the flagship of the admiral in charge of the First Naval District. But it stays at its berth, where thousands of visitors can climb aboard. The young Navy men in its crew are skilled guides. They like to tell visitors about the history of the great old ship. They are very proud to be associated with the most famous ship in American history and like most Americans, they will never forget the contribution it made in winning respect for a new nation.

About the author: Norman Richards grew up in a small New England town. He has always been interested in transportation and its development. A graduate of Boston University's journalism school, Mr. Richards has written more than 100 magazine articles on aviation and travel. He is the author of the recently published book on the history of dirigibles, GIANTS IN THE SKY. As managing editor of MAINLINER, United Air Lines' magazine for passengers, he travels 100,000 miles a year in jets, light planes and helicopters to cover stories.

About the illustrator: Tom Dunnington grew up in Iowa and Minnesota. He began his art training in Indiana and continued it at the Art Institute and the American Academy of Art in Chicago. He has five children, lives west of Chicago in Elmhurst, and works full time as a free-lance artist.